Lerner SPORTS

ALL-STAR SMACKDOWN

SUNISA LEE VS. MARY LOU RETTON

WHO WOULD WIN?

K.C. KELLEY

Lerner Publications ◆ Minneapolis

Lerner Publications Company
An imprint of Lerner Publishing Group, Inc.
241 First Avenue North
Minneapolis, MN 55401 USA

For reading levels and more information, look up this title at www.lernerbooks.com.

Main body text set in Aptifer Sans LT Pro.
Typeface provided by Linotype AG.

Library of Congress Cataloging-in Publication Data

Names: Kelley, K. C., author.
Title: Sunisa Lee vs. Mary Lou Retton : who would win? / K.C. Kelley.
Other titles: Sunisa Lee versus Mary Lou Retton
Description: Minneapolis, MN : Lerner Publications, [2025] | Series: All-star smackdown | Includes bibliographical references and index. | Audience: Ages 7–11 | Audience: Grades 2–3 | Summary: "Sunisa Lee and Mary Lou Retton both captured the imaginations of gymnastics fans. But is one superstar Olympian better than the other? Explore their careers and decide which gymnast stands on top of the podium"—Provided by publisher.
Identifiers: LCCN 2023049776 (print) | LCCN 2023049777 (ebook) | ISBN 9798765625903 (library binding) | ISBN 9798765628140 (paperback) | ISBN 9798765632208 (epub)
Subjects: LCSH: Women gymnasts—United States—Biography—Juvenile literature. | Lee, Sunisa, 2003-—Juvenile literature. | Retton, Mary Lou, 1968-—Juvenile literature. | Olympic athletes—United States—Biography—Juvenile literature. | Artistic gymnastics—History—Juvenile literature.
Classification: LCC GV460 .K45 2025 (print) | LCC GV460 (ebook) | DDC 796.44092/52—dc23/eng/20231027

LC record available at https://lccn.loc.gov/2023049776
LC ebook record available at https://lccn.loc.gov/2023049777

Manufactured in the United States of America
1 – CG – 7/15/24

TABLE OF CONTENTS

Sunisa Lee

INTRODUCTION

TWO GYMNASTICS GREATS

At the 1984 Summer Olympics in Los Angeles, California, US gymnast Mary Lou Retton had to be perfect on the vault. Anything less and the all-around gold medal would go to another gymnast. Retton trailed Romania's Ecaterina Szabo by only .05 points.

Fast Facts

- Mary Lou Retton won five Olympic medals.
- Retton is a member of the US Olympic Hall of Fame.
- Sunisa Lee has won three Olympic medals.
- Lee won gold in the team event at the 2019 World Championships.

The only way Retton could win was with a perfect score of 10. Retton raised her arms over her head. Then she sprinted down the runway.

Retton jumped on the vault and bounced into the air. She twisted her body and did a backward flip. She landed with a thump. Both feet smacked down onto the mat. She had done it! Retton's perfect score had won Olympic gold.

Thirty-seven years later, another US gymnast faced a similar moment. Sunisa Lee led the US women's gymnastics team at the Olympics in Tokyo, Japan. Her grace and control helped her put up great scores. Like Retton, Lee was good at all four gymnastics events.

Mary Lou Retton

Lee stepped up because teammate Simone Biles had pulled out of the team event and all-around. In the team event, Lee had a top score on the uneven bars. That helped win a silver medal for the US.

In the all-around, Lee won gold. She was the first Hmong American to win an Olympic medal. Her story made headlines around the US.

Both Retton and Lee were outstanding athletes and inspired thousands. Who will win this gymnastics smackdown?

Retton on the balance beam at the 1984 Olympics

Lee jumps above the beam at the Olympics in Tokyo in 2021.

CHAPTER 1

Nadia Comaneci won five Olympic gold medals in 1976 and 1980.

THE ROAD TO THE OLYMPICS

Mary Lou Retton was born in a small coal-mining town in West Virginia on January 24, 1968. Her parents sent the active girl to dance classes. Soon she started gymnastics as well. She was inspired by Olympic stars such as Olga Korbut and Nadia Comaneci. Mary Lou loved gymnastics so much that she slept in her gear the night before events.

When she was 14, Mary Lou and her family moved to Houston, Texas, to train with other gifted gymnasts. Moving halfway across the country to live and work with fellow athletes was a big change. They inspired her to improve and be her best.

In Houston, Mary Lou learned to use her natural strength and power. This was a new way to train. Women gymnasts had usually focused on grace and dance-like moves.

Coaches help young gymnasts learn the right moves.

Retton made her move into the top ranks of gymnastics in 1983. She earned a spot in the American Cup in New York City. At 15, no one expected her to win. But she won the all-around, surprising opponents and fans. It was the start of a great run of success.

Later that year, Retton was the first American to win the Chunichi Cup in Japan. In 1984, she won the American Cup again. She also won the US National Championships all-around title.

Retton led the way at the 1984 US Olympic Trials.

Retton's biggest win came at the 1984 US Olympic Trials. She finished with the best score among 24 Americans. The result made her a member of Team USA for the Olympic Games.

But just six weeks before the Olympics, Retton faced a big challenge. She hurt her knee while practicing. Retton had to work fast to get back into shape. She rode a bike, jogged, and swam.

Shortly before the Olympics began in Los Angeles, she tested her knee on a vault. The knee held up. She was okay! Retton was ready to take on the world.

Retton tested her injured kneed with vaults like this one.

Sunisa Phabsomphou was born March 9, 2003, near Minneapolis, Minnesota. She later changed her last name to Lee. The name honored John Lee, her mother's partner who helped raise Sunisa. Some of Sunisa's family members were among many Hmong people who had moved from Laos in southeast Asia to the United States. Many were escaping war in Asia. People in Minnesota welcomed them.

Sunisa started taking gymnastics lessons when she was six. She improved quickly. She was a state champion in her age group within a year.

Sunisa **(left)** ***with John Lee*** **(center)**

Lee shows her moves on the balance beam.

By the time she was a teenager, Lee competed in national events. Like Retton, Lee didn't train the way many other gymnasts did. Most coaches told their gymnasts what to do. Lee's coaches taught her to choose her own goals.

When she was 14, Lee earned a place on the US Junior National Team. She helped the US win a gold medal at the International Junior Cup. A year later, Lee finished third in the all-around at the US Junior National Championships. She was a rising star in gymnastics.

Lee made her big move at the 2019 US National Championships. In the all-around, she came in second to Olympic gold medalist Simone Biles. In the single-event finals, Lee won gold on the uneven bars and bronze in the floor exercise.

Later that year, Lee won all-around silver at the World Championships. Once again, she finished behind Biles. Then, in 2021, Lee earned a spot on the US Olympic team. She headed to Tokyo to compete for her country.

CONSIDER THIS

Retton overcame a knee injury to compete in the 1984 Olympics. Lee recovered from injuries to her foot and ankle the year before she was in the Olympics in 2021.

Lee earned a bronze for this floor exercise at the 2019 US National Championships.

CHAPTER 2

Retton performs at the 1984 American Cup.

GREATEST MOMENTS

In 1983, Retton took part in her first major contest. She flew to Japan to take part in the Chunichi Cup. Athletes from around the world joined her there. She put up top scores in the vault and floor exercise. She impressed judges with her powerful style.

Retton also had excellent scores in the uneven bars and the balance beam. Her total score of 38.85 earned her the gold medal. She was the first American to win this big event.

The next year, Retton dominated the US National Championships. She won the all-around to become a national champion for the first time. She went on to earn gold medals in both the vault and floor exercise.

Retton at the 1984 US Olympic Trials

In June, Retton continued her success. At the US Olympic Trials, she posted the top score. The young gymnast from West Virginia was on her way to the Olympic Games.

CONSIDER THIS

Lee has won five medals at the US National Championships, including two gold. Retton also did well at nationals, earning three gold medals.

Gymnasts at the 2019 US National Championships performed in front of a huge American flag.

Lee took a huge leap forward at the 2019 US National Championships. She and Biles faced off in Kansas City, Missouri. Biles came out on top, but Lee's scores were excellent. She finished only five points behind Biles to earn a silver medal.

In the single-event finals, Lee beat Biles to win the uneven bars gold medal! Lee also earned the bronze medal in the floor exercise. She missed a bronze in the balance beam by only 0.3 points. Lee was a rising star in US gymnastics.

At the 2019 World Championships, Lee earned her first world championship gold medal. She was part of the first-place US team. In the single events, Lee was right behind Biles with a silver in floor exercise and a bronze in uneven bars.

In 2020, Lee had a foot injury. But the Olympic Games were postponed to 2021 because of the disease COVID-19. She recovered from her injury in time to earn a spot on the US Olympic team.

Lee's balance beam work helped the US win the 2019 World Championships team gold.

CHAPTER 3

Retton spins on the uneven bars.

OLYMPIC GLORY

At the 1984 Olympic Games in Los Angeles, the top team did not compete. The Soviet Union was a nation of 15 republics, including Russia. It had won the previous eight gold medals in the team event. But in 1984, the Soviet Union and several other countries did not compete in the Olympics.

Led by Retton, the US gymnastics team stepped up. They earned silver in the team event. It was the US's first team event medal since 1948! Romania won gold.

On August 13, 1984, the top-scoring women from the team event took part in the all-around. After three rounds, Retton trailed a gymnast from Romania. Retton needed a perfect 10 on the final round in the vault. She nailed it! Retton was the first American to win the gold medal in the all-around.

Two days later, Retton won three medals in single events. She won silver in the vault. She also won bronze medals in the uneven bars and floor exercise. Almost overnight, she became one of America's most famous athletes.

An Olympic gold medal earned a big smile from Retton.

Heading into the 2021 Olympic Games in Tokyo, fans expected Simone Biles to win. However, she had to pull out due to health reasons. That opened the door for Lee. Like Retton in 1983, Lee stepped up to the challenge and became a star.

First, Lee and the US won a silver medal in the team event. Lee's score of 15.4 on the uneven bars was the highest score in a single event in the Tokyo competition.

Lee came through with a big score on the uneven bars to help the US win silver.

Then, in the all-round, Lee continued her success. The scoring system had changed since 1984. Gymnasts could no longer earn perfect 10 scores. Lee could not be perfect, but she could still be great.

Lee put up excellent scores in the first three events. In the floor exercise, she put on a great show. After Rebeca Andrade of Brazil made two mistakes, Lee was the winner. Lee finished just 0.135 points ahead of Andrade.

US gymnastics fans were thrilled at Lee's success. Her family and community in Minnesota were especially happy. They held a parade in her honor.

Lee shows her all-around gold medal.

CONSIDER THIS

Comparing scores between Retton and Lee is difficult. Retton earned a single score for each performance. Lee earns one score for difficulty and one for how well she performs. Those points are combined for her final score.

CHAPTER 4

In 2003, Retton* (left) *met with athletes at the American Cup.

AND THE WINNER IS

Retton enjoyed instant fame after winning gold in 1984. She was on dozens of magazine covers. She appeared on many TV shows. She met then US president Ronald Reagan. Along with other Olympians, she took a trip to Disneyland. At the end of the year, *Sports Illustrated* named Retton Sportswoman of the Year.

Retton retired after winning the 1985 American Cup. She was the first gymnast to join the US Olympic Hall of Fame. She was talented, worked incredibly hard, and had a huge impact on her sport. Thousands of young people started taking gymnastics after her Olympics win. Gymnastics clubs grew quickly.

Retton (right) and the 1984 US Olympic team met then US president Ronald Reagan (left).

Lee was one of the athletes inspired by Retton and other US stars. Lee also has an impact beyond the gym. By taking home gold in 2020, she drew attention to the Hmong community in Minnesota and to her new way of training.

Lee continued her career after the Olympics. She earned two college event championships with Auburn University. She also continued training for the 2024 Summer Olympics.

Retton was shorter than Lee. Her style was more powerful. Lee is more graceful, but she is also strong. Both athletes won Olympic gold medals and were good at every gymnastics event. They could both win this smackdown.

It's a close call, but Lee is the winner. Her career has lasted longer than Retton's did. Lee has battled all of the world's best and come out on top. Who do you think the winner is? Consider their stories and make your choice!

Lee loves being part of a team at Auburn University.

At the 2022 national college championship, Lee won the balance beam event.

SMACKDOWN BREAKDOWN

SUNISA LEE

Date of birth: March 9, 2003
Olympic medals: 3
US National Championships medals: 6
World Championships medals: 3

Stats are accurate through 2023.

MARY LOU RETTON

Date of birth: January 24, 1968
Olympic medals: 5
US National Championships medals: 3
World Championships medals: 0

GLOSSARY

all-around: when a gymnast competes in all the events and is given a score in each

balance beam: when gymnasts perform on a 4-inch (10 cm) wide beam

event final: the championship round at a gymnastics competition

floor exercise: when gymnasts perform dance steps and tumbling moves on a 40-square-foot (3.7 sq. m) mat

runway: a long padded area where gymnasts run

team event: when a gymnastics team competes in all the events and is given a score in each

uneven bars: when gymnasts perform on two bars at different heights

vault: when gymnasts launch from a springboard to a vaulting table and then into the air

LEARN MORE

Fishman, Jon M. *Suni Lee.* Minneapolis: Lerner Publications, 2022.

Flynn, Sarah Wassner. *Gymnastics.* Washington, D.C.: National Geographic Kids, 2021.

Goldstein, Margaret J. *Epic Gymnastics Moments.* Minneapolis: Lerner Publications, 2024.

Gymnastics Facts for Kids
https://kids.kiddle.co/Gymnastics

Sports Illustrated Kids: Women's Gymnastics
https://www.sikids.com/tag/womens-gymnastics

USA Gymnastics Hall of Fame
https://usagym.org/halloffame/

INDEX

PHOTO ACKNOWLEDGMENTS

Danielle Parhizkaran-USA TODAY Sports, p. 4; USA Today Sports, p. 5; USA Today Sports, p. 6; Robert Deutsch-USA TODAY Sports, p. 7; AP Photo, p. 8; BearFotos/Shutterstock, p. 9; Ronald C. Modra/Getty Images, p. 10; Focus on Sport/Getty Images, p. 11; Evan Frost/Minnesota Public Radio via AP, p. 12; Melissa J. Perenson/CSM/via AP Image, p. 13; Amy Sanderson/ZUMA Wire/Cal Sport Media via AP Images, p. 14; AP Photo, p. 15; AP Photo, p. 16; Denny Medley-USA TODAY Sports, p. 18; Kunihiko Miura/Yomiuri Shimbun/AP Photo, p. 19; USA Today Sports, p. 20; Darr Beiser-USA TODAY Sports, p. 21; Frank Hoermann/picture alliance/Sven Simon/Newscom, p. 22; Kyodonews/ZUMAPRESS/Newscom, p. 23; AP Photo/Matthew Cavanaugh, p. 24; Dirck Halstead/Getty Images, p. 24; Dirck Halstead/Getty Images, p. 25; Amy Sanderson/ZUMA Wire/Newscom, p. 26; Kyle Okita/Cal Sport Media/Newscom, p. 27; Danielle Parhizkaran-USA TODAY Sports, p. 28; AP Photo/Lionel Cironneau, p. 29.

Cover: AP Photo/Lionel Cironneau (Retton); Robert Deutsch-USA TODAY Sports (Lee).